~ Also by bell hooks ~

When Angels Speak *of* Love

poems

bell hooks

ATRIA BOOKS

New York   London   Toronto   Sydney

ATRIA BOOKS

1230 Avenue of the Americas
New York, NY 10020

Library of Congress Cataloging-in-Publication Data

hooks, bell.
     When angels speak of love : poems / by bell hooks.—1st Atria Books hardcover ed.
          p. cm.
     1. Love poetry. 2. African Americans—Poetry. I. Title.

PS35608.O594W47 2007
811'.54—dc22

2006049882

ISBN-13: 978-1-4516-3975-9

First Atria Books hardcover edition February 2007

10 9 8 7 6 5 4 3 2 1

ATRIA BOOKS is a trademark of Simon & Schuster, Inc.

Manufactured in the United States of America

Designed by Jaime Putorti

For information regarding special discounts for bulk purchases, please contact Simon & Schuster Special Sales at 1-800-456-6798 or business@simonandschuster.com.

for angels who go before,
making ready the way—

The angels are so enamored of the language that is spoken in heaven, that they will not distort their lips with the hissing and unmusical dialects of men, but speak their own, whether there may be any who understand it or not.

—Ralph Waldo Emerson

1.

love go to my heart straight
beat beat
alive and more alive
oh time before words
and i can still remember
each touch
all every bit tenderness
only one pain
a cry to make it be
always endless bliss

2.

in love
there are no closed doors
each threshold
an invitation
to cross
take hold
take heart
and enter here
at this point
where truth
was once denied

3.

and how
she adores me
precious precious
sweet sweet
all favorite things
flesh that is my flesh
bone that is my bone
and we always be one
even at the moment
of heartbreak
surrender and separation
we know
times come again
eternal abiding love
another chance
seduced
she promises me
another chance

4.

in him
my twin likeness
all flesh a mirror
pentimento
palimpsest
all traces
seeds pressed
in flower beds
a diary of enchantment
his hands hold mine
keep me standing firm
ground my heart
the angel eye of love
stands guard
protects our union
we are too much one
too much each other

5.

when he bids me
separate
go home
stop following behind
let there be
time without memory
all is loss
my soul gone
into numb nothingness
my body unable
to know or move
from this strange
forbidden garden
he lures me here
where love
will not come again

6.

amid cornfields
cabbage rows
hot peppers
tall tomato vines
succulent ripe hearts wail
all order
neat in nature
living to give sustenance
for wounded spirits
wild asparagus
honeysuckle trails
hanging borders
eden all would abandon
to not be alone
even in paradise
i dream you are
coming love
to resurrect me
to save me from decay
and lead me home

7.

love is
no soldier of fortune
no assassin
on the prowl
stalking unsuspecting hearts
each evil lurking here
takes any pleasing form
fallen angels
mock nighttime's splendor
unmasking
each remembered
connecting trace

8.

oh love
a serpent to find
in loss keeps
abandoned angel
innocence
set loose
this side of paradise
binds the heart
with promises
just follow
he will guide
lead home
if only he can touch
sweet sacred flesh
if only he can make
secret never to be
seen wounds
if only she will promise
never to forget
if only she always
feels the pain

9.

inside dark rooms
no one sees wounds
raw open quiet places
where love leaves
no trace of remembered bliss
and no one hears
my heart calling
do not forsake me
one more time

10.

bluegrass waterfalls
lingering taste of starch
naked earth clay
damp dark digging
fishing worms wiggle
clear moonshine
dandelion splendor
an unending heat
small wonders
awaken such lovely soul
let sorrow loose
free the heart
in deep red
this is love's memory
a poultice held
next to flesh and wound
a balm to soothe
all pain
to press against hurt

11.

the first taste of death
wets my hunger
i need to live each moment
in that same closing of the eyes
that same ecstasy
let me lie here
in everlasting peace
in love's embrace
let me enter sleep
with dark midnight
as my witness

12.

after slow death
love must clean house
choose memories to keep
and memories to let go
give each lamentation
an ear to hear
a heart to lay rest
let no soul forget
an eternity of desire awaits

13.

my first love
a backwoods man
comes smelling
of wild things
and too long time
apart from the living
armed with gun and game
he brings his lady tender
rabbit possum and coon
all sweet strong meat
aphrodisiacs to stand
against the end of innocence

14.

my daddy
don' love me no mo'
he takes his heavy hand
and hurted me
pain me to my heart
to let me know
i can be his brown sugar girl
no mo'
what happen here
what went wrong
how come
i am all same same
but my daddy change change
take his love away
leave my inside soul
cleared out blank empty
and me with no place
to go forget

15.

hold on
take my hand
let go
on the ride
race you down
hill up hill
dust on dirt road
clinging
let me follow you
anyplace
in love
there is no end
we are glory
everywhere
in nature
a paradise surrounds us
wild tenderness
take hold
loose and let
our spirits soar

16.

big mama coming
bringing love so sweet
a foreign thing
bonbon pretty
pink yellow
and two shades of blue
come to seduce us silly
with pocketbook and pipe
pressed apron and slicked
back covered hair
take us all as we are
embracing bodies in folds of
dark warm woman flesh
this heaven-sent secret
odor of enchantment

17.

don't let
your loving
take too long
you may come
too late
and i'll be gone
don't let
fear
make you stray
don't wait
on heartbreak
to show the way

18.

my heart is burning
in this house
where i dreamed
in the dark
my deepest dreams
shrouded desire in shadows
places the dead used to know
upstairs long
little bed low
quilts from hand-me-downs
curtains hung with faded lace
the smell of tobacco
nightshade and morning cool
this scent love's memory
everything broken and on fire

19.

braided
tobacco leaves
twisted hung
time on the
loosening floor
time stripping
time drying
time turning
sheets of brown
time turning away
and all the time love
the smell of smoke
between us

20.

a palimpsest
of fire
your words
are fingers on my flesh
hands to take
my body
rising heat
touch not
the flame
of this too hot
heavy love
for it will turn
our world to ash
and make the heart
a grave

21.

dark midnight
roaming
seeking a
shoot-and-cut passion
a death
to wound and bind us
the assassin's testimony
i had to kill
to lay bare
the heart
i had to kill
to let go
hold on
be still
eliminate love's trace

22.

love ain't got
no messenger
send death instead
love don't need
no witness
let the spirit testify
'cause it no matter
life or no life
strange heart or
familiar beat
whoever calling
they don't know
how to say my name

23.

love in sweet morning
love in the afternoon
late-night love
in between sheets
terrors and nightmare
love dreaming
a second coming
rescue resurrection
love keeping me safe
every day all day

24.

love don't make no promises
the heart cannot keep
he offers kisses from the divine
nighttime angels
standing by my bed
whispering in my sleep
teaching me dream rhythm flight
all the ways to move
beyond life and death
telling me sweet soul child
only surrender
love will not let you forget

25.

one cannot love
cowboy boots
red plaid vest
white cotton ruffles
and a holster with no gun
one cannot love these
slow killing things
these blue memories
one cannot love
an image
a dead likeness
it will never give back
the real you
or let you see
the inside heart

26.

let me be
a witness to love
stand on the outside
and see tenderness
unbidden
kind words
and a lover's sweet touch
let me be
a witness to love
see each sacrifice surrendered
how patient and joined
such open heart
let me see and then believe

27.

no kind love
would leave me here
take away treasures
strip me bare
of all the soul
holds dear
forsake all just
and fair due
then flaunt
its heady passion
openly offering
the heart's allure
only to seduce and
then betray
only i am not slain
though fallen
for love would never
lead me here

28.

angels hear
how she weeps
in the night
tenderly attend her woe
each dark winged
heavenly creature
comes with thread in hand
ready to mend
this broken heart
gathering bits and pieces
every pain shattered fragment
pierced anew
love's holy grace
render each wound
divine anguish

29.

love
has heard
my cry
and shelters me
not even fear
of death
or the grave
still my courage
crush this yielding heart
or make all yearning flee
within me
every closed door opens
paradise enters
grant lost souls
solace and sanctuary

30.

oh love
he tells me
i don't know
can't understand
never think
don't know how
only that
there is intense connection
strong binding
abiding warmth
oh love
i come to you who know
the way
oh love
i kneel down
and press my face
against the bosom of memory
where i first yearned
and knew then
how to let my hunger speak

31.

love will not let me speak
will not let me seek words to say
how heavy my heart
the way the weight of your body
closes me down
shuts the door
take off your shirt
hang your tie here
just as you like to be
all loose and free again
let me dress you
in a dark blue suit
when you wear it
i remember desire
full and complete
an intensity so hot
i cannot find air
here in this room
where you
do not come again
to lie next to me
after the
heavy work is done

32.

even though
she knows
a terrorist comes
she can bear witness
can tell you by now
we have been
together
our bodies
spying on your love
on naked hands
as they move to touch her
and make her over
another woman
marked by the embrace
of a man
known to leave scars

33.

to cut
and cut
the heart
another weapon
i can use
its pointed sharp edge
the very tip of desire
pierces you
brings you to the
ecstatic red of the cut
and the blood
that is love's last moment
to tarry and sup together
in remembrance

34.

bring me angels
to keep away hurt
shield and solace
offer divine sanctuary
in love there
is no need to find
a hiding place
and when beloved
you come again
i will know your face
and speak your name

35.

saint antonio
oh you who are able
to bring back the lost
i beseech you
he was the only body
i could ever love
like a brother he was to me
he would kiss me
tenderly touch braided hair
and let me put my ear
close to the place
where no heart beats
and there is only the sound
of a closing door
in that place where memory forgets
so there can be no more pain
kneeling with all that remains
left precious and whole
sweet flesh in my mouth
where i call to jesus
and he comes to me

to guard us here
as we search in the dark place
for you beloved
who are able
to bring back the lost

36.

love if you were
a reader of hearts
you would know
such longing
must never speak
or seek a listening here
where he takes my hand
and i am not ready to be
born a child again
not ready to forget
there is no death
not now
all sweetness gone
the hard heart still
and charming allure
all eager to speak
to my heart
to talk its way back in
here let me hurt you
with my sight
hold out your hands

the future tells me
everything is always lost
there is nothing
only departure and ending
it is best to stay silent
and keep away

37.

love
looked down on
belittled judged
and unable to bear
the heart's weight
can never last
for time will make it
tired and worn
it will grow hard
rage will
overcome desire
and we will forget
what it was like
to know each other
without eyes and testimony

38.

sweet sacrifice
a finger in each mouth
to carry away all praise
i have had to offer
body parts
to let go hands that solace
eyes that hold her
captive heart
with just one look
to let go touch
render strange
and unfamiliar
this killing passion

39.

empty now
the red chair
where i sit
to write of love
no naked body easing down
opening hard
in this rocking of
our bodies
as we join
and move again
breast to breast
i face your hunger
wet and in need
we came here always
to this meeting place
where now there is only
silence quiet breathing
and the sound of
words moving against words

40.

if true love died
before we ever had
a chance to see
what it would be
if we were really free
to make promises
and speak the heart
then we would not need
to be sent grace
in innocent flesh
or given sacrifice
i leave a bit of my heart
on this altar
flesh to take home
naked and young
the way we would have been
i leave a taste of mystery
of love undeclared
let him
eat away grief

41.

when angels speak of love
they tell us
all is union and reunion
dying reborn again
there is no separation
no end to paradise
we are always present
the ecstatic moving us
along each current
each wilderness of spirit
a dedicated path

42.

ever dark prince
yearns with all the
passion of the cross
sanctified satanic wish
to seduce and sacrifice
love's innocence
making it serve flesh
kneeling at the phallic altar
drinking in the seed of
his revenge

43.

how hard
and sweet
this taste of flesh
enchanting
chameleon
seductive trace
tenderly taken love
the snake
guarding
the palace of bliss
to enter
there is only
one open door

44.

outside
in the passage
between life and death
love waits
counts in unrecorded rhythm
hours minutes
each moment matters
speak now my heart
say when how
which way
only now
before time is no more

45.

i gave my heart
and in return
a heart is given
no lasting body
no definite trace
strangers kneel
in the same temple of love
i thought my heart
alone belonged
connect the unfamiliar
claim mystery
in deep history
heaven's new frontier
my own and
not my own

46.

love
should not come
in such a way
i cannot know
the heart's yearning
i dreamed a prince
a frog destiny
everything alchemically
turning
into pure gold
love
should not defy desire
make me over
flesh
make me ready
kill the illusion
let truth submit
and every sacred vow
hold fast

47.

every dark prince
courts me with words
tames the imagination
puts his tongue
in my mouth
speaks tenderly
to my heart
to love left lonely
uncovers secrets
becomes the interpreter
of desire
seduces my soul
with each narrative of surrender

48.

every prince
in the book
of love
journeys
from a faraway
dark place
finds an angel
of mercy
to shelter and shield
him from pain
he enters my dreams
tells me
i can find my true desire
if i follow
the heart's labyrinth
show naked courage
and a will to give all
yet when we meet
and i have finally
come home
he is already

leaving
already mapping his return
to the land
where the royal one
sleeps alone in a place
without light

49.

once
only men
could become
angels
offering the promise
of divine love and
eternal bliss
then one by one
they fell from grace
seduced by death's allure
boldly they surrendered
the promise of paradise
claiming pain as their
one true passion
and their only home
the heart forsaken
found in woman
a place to love again
to dream anew
the angelic to herald
the coming of a new world
a new vision

50.

a heady heavy love
speaks my yearning
calls me
to give my all
and seek the place
of no return
to lay bare my heart
for you
to whom i surrender
to you
for whom i wait